You're Leading Now!

A Six-Step Strategy for Building and Leading Dynamic Teams

by Tiffany Timmons-Saab

Illustrated by Amy Koch Johnson

Hardcover ISBN - 978-0-9995556-0-6
Paperback ISBN - 978-0-9995556-1-3
Ebook ISBN - 978-0-9995556-2-0

Leadership.

The word speaks volumes. When you're a leader, you're responsible for so much: productivity, teamwork, morale, and more. When you do it right, the job is incredibly rewarding. If you fail, the consequences can be drastic.

Perhaps you've spent years leading multiple departments and want a fresh perspective. Or maybe you're adding employees to your small business and need to brush up on your management skills. Whatever your situation, your approach to leadership can make or break your success.

I've spent years coaching, consulting, and helping business leaders transform their organizations. Through it all, one of the most important lessons I've learned is that leadership isn't a trait; it's a skill. And like other skills, it can be developed. When presented with leadership challenges, whether you succeed or fail is up to you.

There are two very important things about this book that I hope you'll take to heart.

First, I wrote the book to help you and your team learn how to transform your organization. The information will help you be a better leader, but it's not just for you. I encourage you to share it with your team, giving them a sense of ownership as you work toward your goals together.

Second, it's not just the message that's important. It's also the delivery. I wrote this text in rhyme to help you truly understand and retain its message. Rhyme is a powerful tool, aiding comprehension and memory; it activates the brain in ways that prose doesn't. My hope is that this book and its six steps will help you and your team now and into the future.

Your partner in leadership,

Tiffany

Tiffany Timmons-Saab

Table of Contents

INTRODUCTION

I'm a problem-definer, a problem-solver,
and I like to gift-wrap solutions with ribbons.
My goal is to help you be the best you can be.
My name is Tiffany Timmons.

This book is for you—for you and your team.
As a professional, leader, big scorer, go-getter,
this is your time to fulfill your potential
and unleash your power to do it all better.

This book is unique and its concept is different;
it relies on rhyme and mnemonic device.
It's a pudding-before-sprouts mentality that asks:
Are YOU ready to lead? Are YOU ready to entice?

Let me introduce you to Guy.
Guy is a guy who reminds me of YOU,
a fierce entrepreneur with the best of intentions
for stupendous success and a team that is true.

This is the story of entrepreneurial revolution,
of Guy's troubles and trials and reconstitution,
of his path to goal fulfillment and conflict resolution,
and the tremendous success of his business evolution.

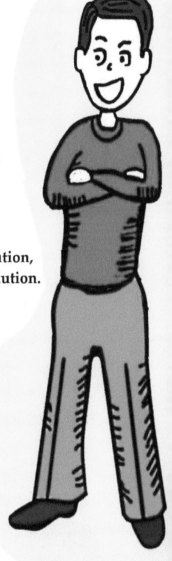

Congratulations: You're Leading Now!

You're leading now!
What will you do?
How will you help your team win
and be successful for you?

This should be easy.
You've dreamt this for years.
Today you're the boss;
you have no fears.

But time ticks on;
things aren't going well.
It is a big challenge
to lead your team to excel.

And when teams don't do
what you tell them to do,
how can that be?
Aren't they inspired by you?

Is "to hope" just the key?

But hope's not a strategy,
although good to hold.
It creates positivity
and helps you be bold.

So what can be done
to turn this around?
To get the results,
can a solution be found?

11

Think you can do it?
Absolutely, you can!
You need the right mindset
and a very good plan.

In six must-do steps,
you can do it for sure.
Create accountability
and your team will endure.

You will need this plan
to help you succeed.
At first it's not easy,
but soon it will be.

The process is simple
but not easy to do.
You can bet on results
if you see it all through.

This plan will need discipline,
design, and desire.
With the right mindset,
your team will reach higher.

If you're open to change
and growing within,
the keys are quite simple
when you're ready to win.

Whether running a company,
branch or small biz,
these Six Steps are proven
to make you a wiz.

And if sales, ops,
or service is your game,
then you're working to win,
and these steps work the same.

Step 1: Vision, Goals, and Planning

Step One: Start with a vision.
This guides your decisions.
It keeps you focused
to stay on your mission.

Break it down into goals;
make sure they are S.M.A.R.T.
All will know how it goes,
and each knows their part.

The roles should be clear.
You'll need to know this.
If you want your team to go high,
help hit their targets, not miss.

Use expectations;
make them standards to reach.
High standards breed excellence,
and that you can teach.

19

You must understand
others and what they need.
Each person is unique;
you will learn what this means.

Integrate the whole person,
not only what you see;
your team's potential is unstoppable
when you understand this key.

A One-on-One's a time to learn
and then to adapt—
to bring out each person's strengths
based on how they interact.

Understanding each member,
where they are and could be,
means development of the individual
and their role on the team.

This sounds easy,
but it takes your whole thought
to connect with each person
because trust can't be bought.

Cross off Step 1;
the fun has begun.
You're leading now...

Step Two is a shortcut
that is easy to take.
"It's to save time," you might say,
but that's a mistake.

Get your team to commit;
don't beat around the bush.
Be direct and clear
and maybe give a gentle push.

We are designed to accomplish,
believe, and achieve.
Make sure they can answer:
"What's in it for me?"

Remember to listen.
Be genuine and sincere—
not overly N.I.C.E.,
thinking it shows you care.

Don't have any F.E.A.R.
to revise and update.
With your team's input,
you'll be ready to race.

And when all agree
on a goal you have set,
your team will be focused.
But don't settle just yet.

Check off Step 2;
you know more than you knew.
You're leading now...

Step 3: Play the Game/Execute

Step three is the time
for your team to show heart.
Execute the plan
right from the start.

You're on the sideline
as you lead them to win.
As much as you want to,
you can't do it for them.

Did you teach them to fish?
Or just how to eat?
You can't hide from results.
There's no way to cheat.

They need to do it.
It's how you all grow.
And if they fail,
they improve what they know.

30

Put all of your efforts
into reaching that goal.
No excuses, no complaints—
show your heart and your soul!

Step 3 is complete,
and you're still on your feet.
You're leading now...

Step 4: Measure Results

Now on to Step Four,
which is keeping the score.
It's seeing your progress
to now from before.

Measure goals in a way
that is open and fair.
A scorecard keeps track
of results you can share.

For what gets measured gets improved,
so numbers are a must.
Define and use it well—
don't let it gather dust.

Celebrate success
along as you go.
Seeing what's done,
watch how it grows.

You've figured out the score
and are done with Step 4.
You're leading now...

Step 5: Debrief/Evaluate Effectiveness

Step Five is debriefing,
so it's time for a meeting.
Identify what's best
and what to do next.

Include your whole team;
leave nobody out.
It's your job to engage.
Leave them with no doubt.

No blames, no excuses,
and no "I didn't knows."
That's really, really not
how a team grows.

Dig for solutions,
empathetic to feelings.

But don't let attitudes
run away with the dealings.

Notice the positive,
no matter how small.
Good builds on good,
and good builds our morale.

Say "Great job!" when it's true,
and say, "Thank you" as such.
No one ever said,
"They thanked me too much!"

Of course, it needs to be earned;
false praise will not do.
Tough love to the end
and they will respect you.

Put ownership on your employees
to help solve the problem.
When they're part of the solution,
the results will be awesome.

You're done with Step 5;
the results have come alive.
You're leading now...

Step 6: Constructive Feedback and Appropriate Consequences

Step Six can slip through;
it's easy to forget.
Because your mind starts to wander
and worry what's next.

Skipping this shows
that you're untrue to your word.
This follow-up is key;
it doesn't make you a nerd!

This is the hard part for most,
but you will need it to grow.
Keep feedback constructive
and make it part of the flow.

Feedback should be designed
to help things improve.
If your plan didn't work,
try new ideas to prove.

Consequences aren't negative—
they're a natural outcome
for what was achieved and
and what didn't get done.

Expect bruises and bumps
along as you go.
Nobody's perfect;
we learn as we grow.

Don't apologize or backtrack.
That's not part of your plan.
It's to truly help people
to grow in this land.

Step 6 was a challenge,
and you made it happen.
You're leading now!

47

Now What ?

You've completed the circle.
Now, what do you do?
You start over again;
it's how you improve.

And what do you risk
if you don't do this?
Your team, your job,
your life you'll miss.

Leaders have choices
between this and that.
Will you hide in the shadows
or go in combat?

To lead by example
and not only in words
means being a leader
that is true to your word.

Be persistent, have discipline,
and always stay true.
On the path you have chosen,
you know what to do.

To be continued...

Here are the steps as a reference to use.
It's a quick glance at the Six Steps you should do.

Step 4 = Measure Results

Step 3 = Play the Game/Execute

Step 2 = Buy-In, Commitment

Step 5 = Debrief/
Evaluate Effectiveness

Step 1 = Vision, Goals,
and Planning

Step 6 = Constructive Feedback
and Appropriate Consequences

Want more?

Order the workbook for You're Leading Now!

Learn more about our training and coaching programs for sales, leadership, presentation skills, and recruiting customization.

Schedule a complimentary session to find out if our programs would work for you.

www.tiffanytimmons.com

The Timmons Group is a leading business transformation firm, energizing growth through cultural change and building human value. Well known for the ability to anticipate, interpret, and facilitate personal and professional growth, the Timmons Group utilizes their proprietary VMT (Variable Mindset Training) and Practice Teams to deliver tangible results.

About the Author

Tiffany Timmons-Saab
Founder
The Timmons Group

With a strong ability to customize and integrate her expertise into various industries, Tiffany has delivered professional coaching, training, and recruiting services to local, regional, and national companies.

As a published author, speaker, and consultant, Tiffany creates training and coaching programs that allow her to adjust messages in real time based on audience participation. Her expressive style has helped business owners focus on results while building human value in their organizations.

She is Ziglar Performance Group and ActionCoach certified. She also holds a Bachelor of Business Administration from the University of Kentucky and a Master of Business Administration.

She currently lives in Scottsdale, Arizona, with her husband and three children.

You're Leading Now!

Bonus Thinkbook

It's great to get ideas,
and action is essential.
Here's a place to take some notes
and unleash your potential.

Need some extra inspiration?
These words will more than serve.
Gain insight from these quotes and stats;
your inner genius will be heard.

It starts with how you think...

No team can outperform the limitations
of its leader. If you want your team to get better,
you have to get better.
(Hanson and Hanson, 2007)

"Don't let what you cannot do
interfere with what you can do."
John Wooden

"There is one cause for failure,
and this is man's lack of faith in himself."
William James

"The man who never alters his opinion is
like standing water and breeds reptiles of the mind."
William Black

Ideas + Actions = Results

"Managers help people see themselves
as they are; leaders help people see
themselves better than they are."
Jim Rohn

"If you want to change others,
you must first change yourself."
Judy Suiter

Forbes magazine states that 85%
of your financial success is due to
skills in human engineering—your
ability to negotiate, lead, sell,
communicate, and work within a team.
15% is due to technical knowledge.

Guard your mind and feed your attitude
with the best you can find; you will be
energized, focused, and ready to solve problems.

"Every hour misspent is lost forever."
George Washington

Ideas + Actions = Results

Step 1:
Vision, Goals, and Planning

"The only thing worse than being
blind is having sight but no vision."
Helen Keller

"Decide what you want, decide what
you are willing to exchange for it, establish
your priorities, and get to work."
H.L. Hunt

"Every time you share your vision, you
strengthen your own subconscious that
you can achieve it."
Jack Canfield

77% of senior managers want to raise their level
of employee engagement, but only 41% of them
communicate personally with employees about
plans and goals on a regular basis.
(Elizabeth, 2014)

Ideas + Actions = Results

To download a FREE Understanding Others
Step-By-Step Communications Guide -
and discover how to get the most out of each
person on your team, go to www.tiffanytimmons.com

The consistently held One-on-One meeting is
probably the most effective way to build deep
trust and rapport (assuming, you, the leader,
listen to the other person).

"Communication is a skill that you can learn.
If you are willing to work at it, you can rapidly
improve the quality of every part in your life."
Brian Tracy

"In preparing for battle I always found that
plans are useless, but planning is indispensable."
Dwight D. Eisenhower

"Then the Lord answered me and said
'Write down the vision clearly upon the tablets
so that one can read it readily.'"
Habakkuk 2:2

Ideas + Actions = Results

Step 2 :
Buy-In Commitment

If you haven't heard them commit,
then they haven't committed. They
are not engaged in the vision.
You are left hoping they will come along.

84% of employees in the U.S. claim
their relationship with their boss
is the top determining factor for whether they try
to move up in the company or find work elsewhere.
(National Business Research Institute)

"If this stat doesn't convince you to explore
solutions to your employee engagement problem,
nothing will; companies with engaged employees
outperform those without up to 202%. That is not a typo."
(Dale Carnegie Institute)

Ideas + Actions = Results

Connect the dots between individual roles and the
goals of the organization. When people see that
connection, they get a lot of energy out of work.
They feel the importance, dignity,
and meaning in their job.
(Blanchard & Blanchard, 2012)

As leaders, 40% of your time is spent listening,
but competency is usually only 25%.
This is a skill that has been forgotten but is needed.
(Burley-Allen, 2007)

"Never tell people how to do things.
Tell them what to do and they will surprise you
with their ingenuity."
General George S. Patton

When John F. Kennedy walked the halls of NASA,
he asked a janitor what he did.
The janitor responded,
"I'm helping to put a man on the moon."

Ideas + Actions = Results

Step 3:
Play the Game/Execute

"It's not whether you get knocked down,
it's whether you get up."
Vince Lombardi

"We grow because we struggle,
we learn and overcome."
R.C. Allen

"Optimism is one quality related to
success more than any other."
Brian Tracy

"The thrill isn't in the winning, it's the doing."
Chuck Noll

"Sometimes you win, and sometimes you learn."
John Maxwell

Ideas + Actions = Results

"In great attempts it is glorious even to fail."
Vince Lombardi

Complaining = Negativity.
Negativity costs the U.S. economy between
$250 and $300 billion every year in lost productivity.
(Gordon, 2008)

90% of doctor visits are stress related,
according to the Centers for Disease Control
and Prevention, and the #1 cause of
office stress is coworkers complaining.
(Gordon, 2008)

"Success happens one day at a time…
day after day…
consistency wins the race in the end…"
Brad Sugars

"Don't count the things you do,
do the things that count."
Zig Ziglar

Ideas + Actions = Results

Step 4:
Measure Results

"What gets measured gets done;
what gets measured and fed back gets done well;
what gets rewarded gets repeated."
John E. Jones

In the business world, measurement accelerates
learning and stimulates innovation.
Clear measures help people move toward a goal,
giving them tangible feedback on
their innovation and efforts.
(Hapst, 2008)

A KPI is a Key Performance Indicator.
They must always be easy to understand,
be relevant, and give the holder of the KPI
the ownership to improve it.

Ideas + Actions = Results

Celebrating progress is fundamental in the
psychology of change.
(Kelly, 2017)

"Inspect what you expect."
Zig Ziglar

Numbers create accountability.
Accountable people appreciate numbers.
Numbers create clarity and teamwork.
You can solve problems faster.
(Wickman, 2012)

Failure is a part of progress, not a final outcome.
(Kelly, 2017)

Ideas + Actions = Results

Step 5:
Debrief/Evaluate Effectiveness

"Don't find fault, find remedy."
Henry Ford

"Honest differences are often a healthy sign of progress."
Mahatma Gandi

"Praise only works with three types of people:
men, women, and children."
Unknown

"It is the front-line staff who know
what needs to be fixed and how to do it."
Quint Studer

Ideas + Actions = Results

People will do their jobs because they get paid.
They will do it better—and stay with you for the
long run— when they feel appreciated.

"A word of encouragement during a
failure is worth more than an hour of
praise after success."
Unknown

"Nothing pains some people more than having to think."
Martin Luther King

"When obstacles arise you change your direction
to reach your goal. You do not change your
decision to get there."
Zig Ziglar

Ideas + Actions = Results

Step 6:
Constructive Feedback &
Appropriate Consequences

"Words may show a man's wit,
but actions his meaning."
Benjamin Franklin

"Criticize if the performance deserves criticism,
but remember to praise the performer.
Criticize in private, praise in public."
Zig Ziglar

"The most valuable of all talents is that of
never using two words when one will do."
Thomas Jefferson

"The challenge of leadership is to be strong,
but not rude; be kind, but not weak; be bold,
but not bully; be thoughtful, but not lazy,
be humble, but not timid; be proud, but not arrogant;
have humor, but without folly."
Jim Rohn

Ideas + Actions = Results

Too many negative interactions compared
to positive interactions at work can decrease the
productivity of a team, according to
Barbara Fredrickson's research team
at the University of Michigan.
(Gordon, 2008)

For a FREE Step-By-Step Guide to
Giving Constructive Feedback,
visit www.tiffanytimmons.com

Positivity only works when it is sincere and honest.
(Blanchard, 2002)

Teams are the primary unit of performance
for increasing numbers [profits] in organizations.
(Katzenbach & Smith, 1992)

Ideas + Actions = Results

Leadership Lifestyle Choices

Ancient wisdom:
Test everything and retain what works.

"The universe rewards those who take action
differently than those who don't."
Eric Lofholm

"Things do not change, we change."
Henry Thoreau

"Great things are not done on impulse,
but by a series of small things brought together."
Vincent Van Gogh

"The best thing about the future is that it
comes only one day at a time."
Abraham Lincoln

"There is a choice you have to make,
in everything you do. And you must always
keep in mind, the choice you make makes you."
Anonymous

Ideas + Actions = Results

References

Blanchard, K. H., Ballard, J., Thompkins, C., & Lacinak, T. (2002). Whale Done!:
The Power of Positive Relationships. New York: Simon & Schuster Adult Publishing Grou

Blanchard, K., & Blanchard, S. (2012).
Do your people really know what you expect from them?, Fast Company. From
https://www.fastcompany.com/1767714/do-your-people-really-know-what-you-expect-then

Burley-Allen, M. (2007). Listening:
The Forgotten Skill: A Self-teaching Guide. New York: Coach Series.

Elizabeth. (2014).
Why employee voice results in employee engagement #infographic.

Employee Engagement,
http://www.thesocialworkplace.com/2014/02/why-employee-voice-results-in-employee-
engagement-infographic/

Gordon, J. (2008).
The No Complaining Rule: Positive Ways to Deal with Negativity at Work.
Chichester, United Kingdom: Wiley, John & Sons.

Gordon, J. (2010). Soup:
A Recipe to Nourish your Team and Culture. Chichester, United Kingdom: Wiley,
John & Sons.

Hanson, T., & Hanson, B. Z. (2007).
Who Will Do What by When? How to Improve Per-formance, Accountability and
Trust with Integrity. Wayne, PA: Power Publications, Inc.

Harpst, G. (2008).
Six Disciplines Execution Revolution: Solving the One Business Problem that
Makes Solving All Other Problems Easier. New York. Six Disciplines Publishing.

Katzenbach, J. R., & Smith, D. K. (1992).
The Wisdom of Teams: Creating the High-Performance Organization. Boston,
MA: Harvard Business School Press.

Wickman, G. (2012). Traction:
Get a Grip on Your Business. Dallas, TX. BenBella Books.

Additional Resources:

Journal of Leadership Studies

National Business Research Institute